PROPERTY OF WAYNE COUNTY
INTERMEDIATE SCHOOL DISTRICT
CHAPTER 2, P.L. 97-35

GESU SCHOOL LIBRARY
DETROIT, MICH. 48221

KOALAS

KOALAS

Patricia Hunt

Illustrated with photographs

DODD, MEAD & COMPANY
New York

A SKYLIGHT BOOK

ILLUSTRATION CREDITS

Australian Information Service Photograph, page 14, 15, 18, 19, 23, 24, 32, 33, 38; Qantas Airways, 43; San Diego Zoo Photo, 1, 2, 6, 8, 11, 13, 16, 17, 21, 25, 27, 30, 36, 40, 41, 45.

Copyright © 1980 by Patricia Hunt
All rights reserved
No part of this book may be reproduced in any form
without permission in writing from the publisher
Printed in the United States of America

3 4 5 6 7 8 9 10

Library of Congress Cataloging in Publication Data

Hunt, Patricia.
Koalas.

Includes index.
SUMMARY: Examines the behavior of koalas in
their natural habitat and the attempts
to preserve them from extinction both in the wild
and in zoos.
1. Koalas—Juvenile literature.
[1. Koalas] I. Title.
QL737.M39H86   599.2   80-13717
ISBN 0-396-07849-4

*For my fourth grade class at
Most Holy Trinity School*

Gum Drop became an orphan koala at the age of three months. When his mother died, he was still too young to be ready to take care of himself. Born at the San Diego Zoo, he had lived with his mother, snug and well fed, till the tragedy occurred.

But Gum Drop was lucky. Dr. Jane Meier, a veterinarian at the zoo, quickly offered to become his foster mother. It was a big challenge, for few people had been successful in hand-raising such a tiny koala. For fear of his getting an infection from other wild animals at the zoo, Dr. Meier decided that Gum Drop would have to share her home—and her time—for the next six months.

Since koalas are nocturnal—that is, they normally sleep by day and are active at night—Dr. Meier now went on

Opposite: Gum Drop

Dr. Jane Meier with Gum Drop *and Springer spaniel,* Brave

twenty-four-hour duty. Each morning she would bring Gum Drop to the zoo's hospital where she worked. He would sleep through most of the day, tightly clutching his own stuffed teddy bear for comfort. Then, when her day's work was done, Dr. Meier would gather together a huge armful of eucalyptus leaves to take home with Gum Drop. (These leaves are the only food a koala ever eats.) After some playful attention in the early evening, Gum Drop was given a pile of leaves to munch. While he was occupied, Dr. Meier would try to catch a few hours' sleep. But it was never for too long. Gum Drop soon developed a huge appetite that kept him chewing mounds of leaves most of the night.

By the time Gum Drop was nine months old, he had grown big enough and strong enough to join the other koalas at the zoo. Dr. Meier's duties as a foster mother were finally over. Today Gum Drop is a healthy young koala. But he still remembers his foster mother. When she drops by to see him, Dr. Meier stretches out her arms and Gum Drop climbs up into them and puts his own arms affectionately about her neck.

What Is a Koala?

A full-grown koala is about two feet long but looks bigger because it is covered so thickly with soft, gray-brown fur. Koalas have round faces with saucer-sized ears and long, black, rubbery-looking noses. They have only a stump where a tail might be.

Anyone who sees a live koala has an almost irresistible urge to pick it up and squeeze it. Koalas tend to invite such a squeeze by looking directly at strange creatures with bright expressions of good will. Of course, not all koalas are alike. Some can be quite cranky.

In spite of being round and bouncy-looking, koalas are good swimmers if the need arises. When they emerge from the water, they shake themselves energetically, like a dog, to dry their fur, and their large ears slap back and forth against their heads.

Normally, koalas are never in a hurry. When sitting up in trees (as they do most of the time), they resemble stuffed teddy bears. But koalas are not bears at all. Scientifically, they are classified as *Phascolarctos cinereus*, a quite different animal altogether. Koalas are marsupials, which means that the female has a pouch, or flap of skin, across her stomach. This pouch encloses the glands, or teats, through which she feeds her newborn infant, and provides a safe place for the baby until it is more fully

Opposite: Koalas have saucer-sized ears and black, rubbery-looking noses.

developed. Young koalas—like all young marsupial animals—are very tiny when born and very underdeveloped. They are worm-sized, have no fur at all, and only a mouth, nose, and forelegs. But as soon as they are born they crawl along the mother's fur and into her pouch.

Koalas usually have only one baby every other year, but —in very rare instances—a mother may have twins. After many months of growing inside its mother's pouch, the baby koala pops its head out of the opening, looks around, and finally crawls out into the world.

Where Do Koalas Live?

Koalas are found naturally only in Australia. They live in scattered sections of forest that run from north to south along the eastern side of Australia. Most Australian mammals—animals that nurse their young—are marsupials with pouches, like the koala. These pouched mammals were among the first mammals to evolve on earth centuries ago when dinosaurs lived. The small marsupials of these early times found their way to the huge southern landmass of the world that at that time included Australia. Then,

Tree kangaroos of Australia

after changes and shifts in the earth, Australia was cut off and became the island continent it is today.

For millions of years the marsupials had this new continent to themselves. They developed and branched out into 150 different species. They became eight-foot tall kangaroos, leaping wallabies, long-nosed bandicoots, bur-

A hairy-nosed wombat

A short-nosed bandicoot

A kangaroo with her baby in her pouch

rowing wombats, strange cuscuses, the koalas, and all sizes of marsupial cats and mice. Elsewhere in the world most of the marsupials died out. Other animals pushed them aside in the competition for food and living space. There are still a few in South America, but in North

America the only marsupial that exists today is the opossum. Australia can be called the "land of living marsupials."

The Daily Routine

As each evening begins, the adult koala yawns itself awake, and gets ready for a night of eating. After sleeping all day in one tree, it may decide it wants to eat the leaves of another tree. To reach the ground, the koala will carefully back down, gripping the tree trunk with the

Opossums—the only marsupials found in North America.

A close-up of a koala's forepaw

sharp nails on its forepaws and hind paws. Then it looks around, smells the air for the scent of tasty leaves, and chooses an eating tree. It gives a small leap up the base of the tree, then walks up with the surety of a telephone repairman. Finally settled onto a branch, the koala carefully pulls off one leaf, smells it, and either drops it to the ground as unacceptable or puts it in its mouth and starts chewing. The koala will keep stuffing its mouth till its

Koalas are able to climb trees quickly.

cheek pouches puff out farther and farther. A feeding koala can look as if it had a case of the mumps.

The trees where most koalas live are eucalyptus trees, also called gum trees. There are at least 350 different kinds of gum trees, but the koala only eats the leaves of about

Koalas eat only eucalyptus leaves.

twenty or so species, and only relishes the leaves of about five. All gum tree leaves are very tough and leathery, and it is not known if any other creatures want them, or are able to digest them. The koala's digestive system is especially adapted for these leaves. Inside its body it has an expandable appendix that is four times the animal's own length. One section, called the *cecum*, is able to expand six inches and serves as a storage area while the tough leaves are being digested. In one night's feeding a koala will put away at least two-and-a-half pounds of leaves. No wonder it needs such a long appendix!

Koalas seem to be finicky eaters when selecting leaves, but for good reason. The young leaves of certain species of gum trees are filled with too much *hydrocyanic* acid. If the koala eats too many of these young leaves, it becomes poisoned and can die. By smelling the leaves first, the koala can tell if the leaf has too much acid. The gum leaves are also very oily and this oil makes all koalas smell like cough drops. Koalas are not bothered by parasites as other animals are because of this medicine-like smell.

Usually there is only one koala to a tree, since they are

Mother koala eating while baby sniffs leaves.

not too sociable with one another. Groups of koalas that know each other form a loose community and may all feed near one another in nearby trees. A full-grown male is the head of the community and keeps other full-grown males away from the trees he considers his home territory. Several females usually take up residence in his trees and they are considered his harem. But even within the little community of koalas, the rule is usually "don't come too close"—except between mother and young, of course.

The koala group stays around a good leafy food supply for some time. When the eating gets sparse, the adult male descends from a tree and starts on a quest for a new home area of eating trees. He walks along the ground with his feet splayed out like a little clown. The rest of the group gradually follows him to wherever he finds a new grove of trees in which to take up residence.

In between feasting on leaves—which goes on most of the night—koalas may put in a little time napping or

Snowy (below) is a white koala at Australia's Taronga Park Zoo. His mother (above) is scratching herself.

grooming themselves. A koala will smooth out the fur on its back by using the claws on its hind paws like a comb. To smooth out the hair high on its back, the koala will swivel its hind leg up and over its back. When it does this it looks like a hinged toy.

Finally the nighttime comes to an end and as daylight

When sleeping, koalas usually secure themselves in the fork of a tree.

Snoozing. If not perched securely, a koala may fall out of a tree when sleeping.

sifts down through the leaves, it is time to bed down again. Usually a koala will settle into a wide fork in the branches of a tree, propping its rear securely into the fork, and then just letting its head nod. Koalas have been known to fall out of a tree when fast asleep if their perches were not secure. If one does fall, the koala is rarely hurt. It just goes *bump*, shakes its head, and climbs back aloft.

A koala's life is largely spent in the treetops, eating and sleeping in a leafy world of its own. Koalas all take life easy. They move slowly and rarely hurry. A contented koala always appears to have all the time in the world.

Male Koalas

When a male koala reaches three or four years of age, he is fully grown and grumpy. He is now an important member of the koala community. He is less tolerant of everything, especially other male koalas. He picks out his area of trees uninhabited by other koalas and claims it for his own for the time being. Now he wants peace and quiet in his part of the forest.

The mature male has a little diamond-shaped gland on his chest that gives off a distinct musty odor. Wherever he goes he leaves an aerial odor trail throughout the trees that tells the world he lives there and that discourages other males from dropping in.

Several females usually take up life in a particular male's

A group of koalas in a tree. Koalas are lively at night, but tend to sleep by day.

territory. They, along with their subsequent young, are his group. He totally ignores the young, but does keep an eye on "his" females.

There is nothing more formidable than when one mature koala male confronts another in a tree, often by accident. The growls start immediately, seemingly rising up from the very bottom of their stomachs. The intruder backs down the tree in haste. Occasionally he is not so easily discouraged and a noisy fight can take place. The "owner" of the tree usually wins. Once the fight is over, he will cry angrily to himself awhile, indicating his extreme displeasure that any other male koala would dare to bother him. Rarely, a young, strong male koala will push an old tired koala out of his claimed territory in the forest. When this happens, the old fellow limps off to live alone.

In the spring of the year (October in Australia, which has seasons reversed from our own) the male koala becomes very noisy and very feisty. It is mating time. He throws back his head and calls loudly and hoarsely for the females to come to his tree. For his size, he probably has the harshest call in all of Australia. If another male is nearby, there may be "courting" fights on the ground between them over the females. The two will bite and scratch, roll over and over, screaming in their anger, until one scuttles away, the loser. The male gets a lot of exercise at this time of year, protecting his females and home trees. But, after a few weeks, all the excitement is over and the males settle down to a life of quiet eating once again.

Mother and Baby

By the time she is four years old, a female koala is mature. Only thirty days after mating, she will give birth to a baby. As soon as it is born, the naked, blind, pink baby koala crawls through its mother's fur till it reaches her pouch. Once inside the pouch, the young koala anchors itself by its mouth to a teat and nurses. The infant stays inside its mother's pouch for at least six months. A koala usually has only one baby at a time.

It is very difficult to tell whether a female is carrying a young one in her pouch or not. Only when a furry little head appears at the opening, at about six or seven months, does anyone get a look at the koala baby. By this time the pouch is getting to be a tight fit for the young koala and it crawls out. Usually the first place it stays is right up on its mother's back. There, tightly clutching her fur, it rides around piggyback. After a while it gingerly

Koala babies usually ride piggyback.

tries to sit on a branch by itself. If it becomes frightened, it will wail just like a human baby and quickly crawl back into mother's pouch for safety. As it watches its mother nibble on leaves, it tries a bite or two and gradually learns to chew leaves. But even when it is almost a year old and nearly as big as its mother, it will stick its big head inside her pouch and try to nurse again.

Mother and young sleep and eat together for about six months after the baby has emerged from the pouch. Then gradually the youngster starts wandering off on its own. Young females usually move into a group of trees held as a territory by a mature male. The young male koalas hang around with their mothers a lot longer—sometimes two years. But by then their father tends to get very annoyed. For the first time he does pay attention to them; it's time for them to move into their own piece of forest. If they don't understand his growls and grumbles, the male will step up his "get moving" campaign by giving them a sharp cuff. And so, life with mother finally comes to an end for them, too.

Dangers and Hazards

Koalas, which can live to be twenty years old in the wild, have little to fear from natural predators. When the marsupial population more or less had Australia to themselves, there were few carnivorous (meat-eating) animals that preyed on the koala. The first people to arrive in Australia brought a doglike creature with them which later developed into the wild dog called the dingo. This animal did prey on some koalas. When the first European settlers came to Australia in the eighteenth century, they brought with them domesticated dogs. Dingos have just about died out, but domestic dogs are everywhere today and can be a problem for koalas.

The koalas are usually safe, high in their trees, but when they change feeding areas and come down to the ground, trouble can arise. The fearless koala will amble along a paved road if it comes to one, not realizing that dogs and automobiles are killers. If a dog starts to chase a grounded

Australian dingos—predators of the koala.

Koalas are in danger when on the ground.

koala, the normally slow-moving marsupial will break into a canter. It may not have time to spring up into a tree immediately. Instead, the koala will get its back to the tree and face its enemy. The dog snarls and nips, but a strong and wily koala will sit on its haunches and use its front claws as weapons. Often it can wound a dog sufficiently so that it has time, finally, to turn and scramble up the tree to safety.

Far more dangerous to koalas are periodic forest fires that occur and have occurred through the centuries. As the trees erupt into flame, almost within seconds, many koalas can be burned to death. Those that realize the danger before the fire reaches their trees try to escape, but sometimes a whole forest can become a trap of fire. Those koalas that survive a fire must migrate from their blackened and leafless homes to a totally new area that may be miles away. Often weak from hunger in such a situation, they may not reach a new home area before they die.

Man as Enemy or Friend

Up to a century ago, except for periodic fires and natural diseases, koalas had little to fear. It is estimated that in 1788 when the first Europeans settled in Australia, there were millions of koalas in the forest that almost covered the eastern coast. In the 1880's man became a danger that threatened their survival. First, of course, many of the forested areas were cleared, leaving them less area in which to live. But far worse than this hazard was the fact that koalas possess such a soft fur. There was a large market abroad for this fur. Killing koalas for their fur soon became commonplace.

Almost defenseless, the small koalas would cling tightly to the branches of trees in a perfect position to be shot or netted. They had no instinct of fear that told them to run. Soon millions of koala pelts were being shipped abroad and whole populations of koalas disappeared. Alaska became one of the major markets for their fur pelts, which were used to make fur hats. In one year over two million skins were exported to Alaska just from the northern area of Australia alone.

Finally, some Australians realized there would be no more koalas if the killing wasn't stopped. Laws were passed and, at last, in the 1930's, the killing was over,

A koala sitting defenseless in a tree.

just in time. Even then the danger had not passed totally, since fires and stress were now major threats to the very small numbers of koalas that remained.

Australian authorities decided that the best way to protect the koala was to create fire-free, guarded sanctuaries, where the koalas could live in safety. Game department experts were able to breed koalas on several small uninhabited islands, building up the population of koalas in these wild sanctuaries. The breeding programs were so successful that they released many young koalas into these new protected areas.

By the 1970's Australia declared that the koala was no longer an endangered species. Now the only problem that remains is keeping the sanctuaries from becoming overcrowded. With less space to move about in, the koalas, if confined to one area too long, can eat the trees bare. The game department sometimes has its hands full, especially when it has to transfer some of the koalas from one place to another to relieve the strain on the food supply. In capturing koalas for relocation, the wardens must be very gentle. It is easy enough to net the koalas and move

Koala and baby in the Tidbinbilla Nature Reserve in Australia.

them, but it must be done expertly. If there is too much stress given the koalas when they are captured and released, they can sometimes die just from the trauma of the experience.

But there is no question that the comeback of the koala has been a major triumph of conservation. In fact, the Australians are so proud of their koalas that they have become a symbol for Australia, replacing the kangaroo.

Koalas in the United States

Koalas never existed anywhere in the world but Australia. But once the world had a look at koalas, attempts were made to add them to zoo collections the world over. Unfortunately for these pioneer koalas shipped to Europe and the United States, none of them survived for long. In these early days no one knew much about the needs of a koala, especially their peculiar eating habits. Even when gum tree leaves were imported, they were never varied enough to sustain the koala.

There has proved to be one exception. The San Diego Zoo in Southern California is famous for its koala collection, the only one that exists today outside Australia. Luckily the California climate is just right for growing gum trees. In addition to some groves of wild eucalyptus planted years ago, the zoo maintains its own plantations of gum trees, just to be sure their little prizes have a good and varied supply of leaves.

Gum Drop in his home at the San Diego Zoo.

The first koalas arrived at the zoo in 1959. There were two females (each with an infant in her pouch) and one male. The zoo has had its ups and downs in keeping koalas. Today it has a special rustic enclosure outdoors as well as

Koobor with his mother, Matilda.

TV-monitored rooms inside. One room is a special breeding room from which the public is excluded. There are six koalas in the exhibit today. Two of the six are youngsters —Koobor (which means "koala boy" in the native tongue of the Australian aborigines) that was born in 1978, and Gum Drop that was hand-raised and is now reaching maturity. The zoo also believes that one of its females is currently carrying a baby in her pouch.

"I Hate Qantas"

Probably the most famous koala in the United States was Teddy, a TV and commercial star that lived at the San Diego Zoo. Qantas, the Australian airline, decided to use a koala as its symbol. Knowing that the appealing koala was in reality an animal that liked to be left alone, they decided to tell the world how much the koala probably hated Qantas for bringing tourists to Australia to disturb its peace and quiet. To start their campaign on TV and make other advertisements for magazines back in 1967, they went to San Diego looking for a "star." Teddy proved to be just right, a grumpy but lovable-looking koala. He was handled with much affection. He never learned to act; he was just himself. But the directors would put Teddy in the seat of a Qantas plane, or in a rowboat, or on an airline runway, and have him say (through a human voice,

Teddy of Qantas fame

of course), "I hate Qantas." He was a hit. Teddy died in 1976 after a most successful career. Subsequently many other koalas, primarily in Australia, have been used as stars for commercials. San Diego no longer allows its koalas to be starred, for fear it may upset them too much.

Koalas Do Have a Future

There are so many endangered creatures in the world today, that it is heartening to know the koala is not one of them. By a lot of effort, and the education of the public, Australia was able to turn around a situation that could have meant the extinction of the koala. But instead, it is possible today to visit Australia and watch koalas in the wild reserves or in zoo collections. They number in the tens of thousands which means, with good management, we need have no fear for the future of the koala. The gentle marsupial that has survived for millions of years now has hope of surviving well into the next century.

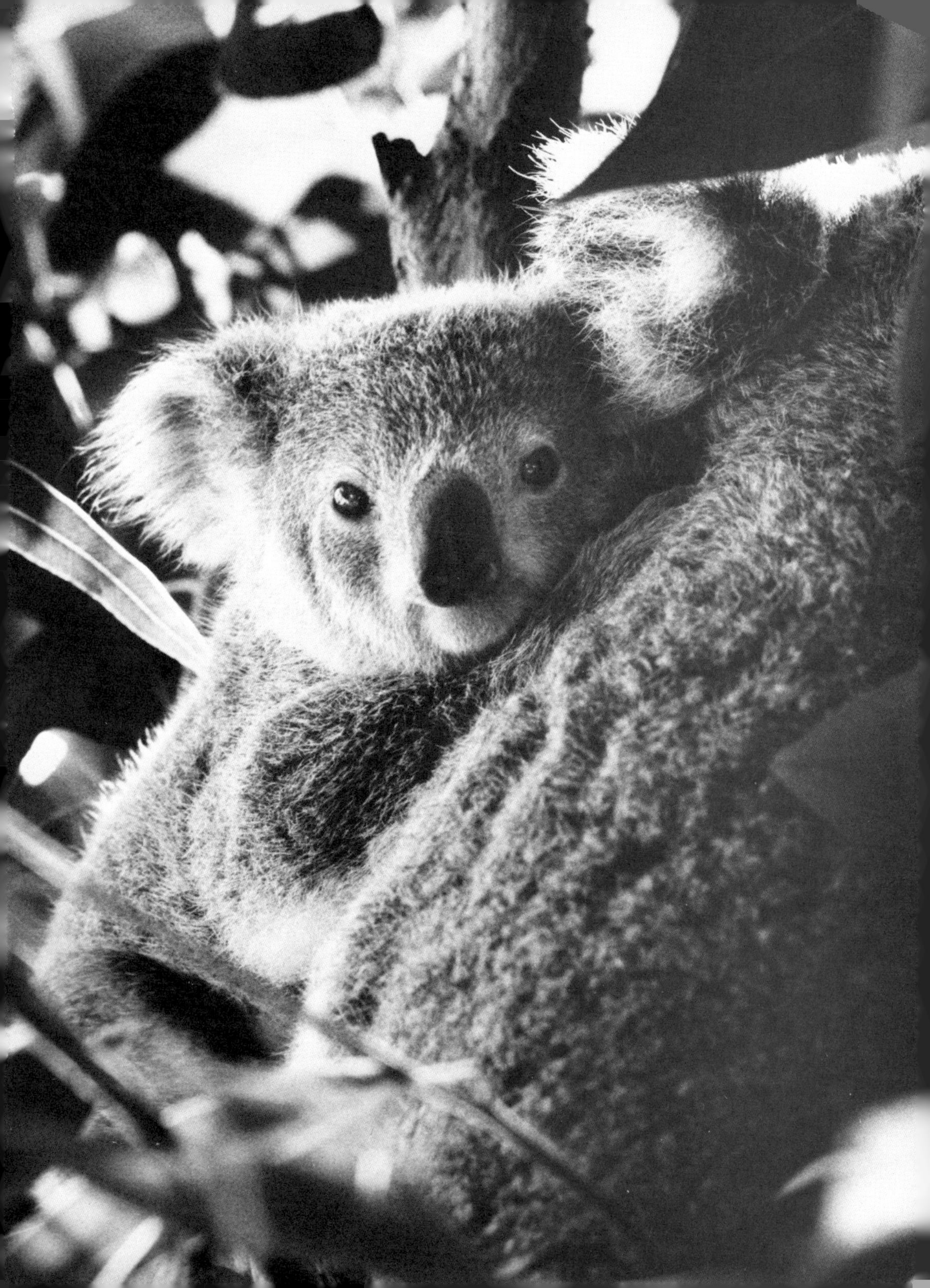

INDEX

Australia, 12, 13, 34, 35, 37, 38, 39, 42, 43, 44

Bandicoots, 13, 14
Birth, 12, 29
Breeding programs, 37

Climbing, 16–17, 18, 34
Communities, 22, 26–27
Cuscus, 15

Description, 9, 10, 11, 12
Digestion, 20

Eating habits, 8–9, 16, 17–18, 19–20, 21, 22, 30
Eucalyptus, 8–9, 18, 19, 20, 38

Fighting, 28–29
Future, 44

Grooming, 23, 24
Gum Drop, 7–9, 40, 42

Habitat, 12
Hazards, 32–35, 37, 38
Home range, 20, 22, 26, 29

Infection, 7

Kangaroos, 13, 15
Koobor, 41–42

Lifespan, 31

Marsupials, 10, 12, 13, 14, 15, 16
Matilda, 41
Mating, 28–29

Maturity, 26, 29, 31
Meier, Dr. Jane, 7–9

Nails, 17
Nocturnal, 7, 27
North America, 15–16

Odor trail, aerial, 27
Opossum, 16

Pelts, 35
Piggyback, 29, 30
Play, 8
Population, 35, 37
Pouch, 10, 12, 29, 40, 42
Predators, 31–32, 33–34

Qantas, 42, 43, 44

Sanctuaries, 37, 38, 44
San Diego Zoo, 7, 39, 40–42
Scientific name, 10
Size, 9
Sleeping, 16, 22, 24–26
Sounds, 28, 30, 31
South America, 15
Swimming, 10

Teddy, 42, 43, 44
Temperament, 10

United States, 39, 42

Wallabies, 13
Wombats, 14, 15

Young, 12, 20, 22, 23
  appearance, 12, 29
  birth, 12, 29
  nursing, 10, 29, 30

About the Author

Patricia Hunt was nature editor for *Life* magazine for about twenty years, until they shut down in 1971. She then worked for Time-Life books as a picture editor.

In addition to teaching the fourth grade at a Long Island school, she is Nature Editor for *SuperMag*, a children's magazine, and nature consultant for *Life*.

This is her first book for children. An animal lover, she now lives on Long Island with her cat, Jo-Jo.

**PROPERTY OF WAYNE COUNTY
INTERMEDIATE SCHOOL DISTRICT
CHAPTER 2, P.L. 97-35**